Earth Messages
of the Love Energy

MESSAGES OF LOVE AND GUIDANCE CHANNELLED FROM
THE CIRCLE OF THE LIGHT BY KAY MEADE

Kay Meade & Peter Ashley

Earth Message Press
earthmessagepress@clear.net.nz
www.earthmessagepress.com

ISBN   978-0-473-18504-6

Cover illustration   Denise Durkin, Illustration Wish, Wellington
Copy editing and design Flying Frog® , Paraparaumu Beach

This book is dedicated to those unseen spirit guides, helpers and angelic beings who are always there to assist us when we ask for help through prayer or meditation

Contents

Introduction

The messages of love and guidance contained in this book are from beings in the higher spiritual realms who call themselves 'The Circle of The Light of The Love Energy'. They say that they wish to spread and increase love on Earth.

The messages were channelled by Kay Meade, a trance medium living in New Zealand. The messages have been received on a regular basis since mid 2009 and continue to be received to this day.

As a trance medium, Kay does not remember what she has said during channelling. Her words are recorded electronically and Peter transcribes them when the session is over.

The messages are presented in the order received and have been written down as they were given. To preserve authenticity, minimal editing has taken place. Thus the grammar is imperfect in places and some words are unusual.

The original recorded messages were often full of emotion, which is lost when the messages are transcribed. Kay was often in tears when channelling.

The several different spiritual guides that Kay channels have distinct voices, personalities and mannerisms, but all are saddened at how we treat each other and the Earth. They say their help and love would be freely given, if only we would ask. They see these messages as a catalyst for change, helping the transition to a world based on love.

A request for help

This was one of the early messages that Kay channelled.

Please help us. We come to you. We ask you to be a deliverer of our words. We know we are connecting.

Time – time to spread the awakening words are now – Love and Light.

We have messages, we ask that you connect with us regularly. We so need a channel to pass on what we need to say. Our messages are of the Love Energy, it really is so needed now. We know we have spoken about it before, but we need to expand on this message. It needs to be released. This energy is for all – we need it to flow.

Kay was shaking with the amount of energy that she was channelling so Peter asked the spirit guide to help balance the energy. Another voice came through.

Good connection now! I am a different energy from previous, but part of the same Circle of Light that is Group Soul of the Love Energy.

Love Energy should be seen as golden in colour. It radiates from the core of your being. It is centred and comes from above the crown into the crown and centres throughout and is the spirit within. This is the connection you have to the Divine without and all around.

Ask through prayer to be drawn into the connectedness of the Whole. The Whole gives all that is needed to nourish, teach, heal and embrace the essential part of you.

Kay, we thank you for allowing us to use your body and your voice to give this message. Please keep this channel open. Please set aside time in your life for us to come. We have the purest of energy that we need you to be the vehicle to spread and impart such an important message to Earth at this time. We know it is unusual, maybe seen as odd, but is truly mystical and is from the highest of energies. We ask you to please allow this pure essence to flow.

Sit and allow this energy to enter and then do whatever you feel you need to do to allow the energy to flow through you. The energy is enormous so you may not want to sit, you may want to use all your physical attributes to impart our message. That is fine – just allow it to happen, the energies will settle and you will be more accepting, controlling of the force so that you will be able to talk to people without the movements, but there will be a knowingness on your part and on the part of your audience that it is Spirit talking.

Connection – connection is the most important. Time for connection. Time to reach for us. You are reaching physically now (Kay had been stretching her arms up towards the ceiling) but reach, reach with the innermost Sacred Energy.

Sacred Energy is the connection we need. Shine with the Sacred Energy. The beauty of the Sacred Energy illuminates all.

Kay, breath it in, draw it close, be anointed and then allow this energy that anoints you to anoint others. Absorb the energy now, allow it to penetrate every part of your being and connect with us again.

Confident that you will. Willing as a clear channel, sanctified by the Divine for the Earth Messages of the Love Energy.

Thank you. We go now. We leave the Love of God with you.

Please connect with us again. Take our request seriously, be the willing channel that is asked of you.

On another occasion Kay channelled the following message.

All messages received are genuine, full of importance, and we ask that their meaning is expressed as given. Genuine in every way – they are. Much trust is needed now to expand the circulation of all information. No more doubting of the whereabouts of the information.

Rest assured the words are from us – carry genuine codes of what is needed now. Some will read and not understand. Some will listen and not hear. But those who register will gain and benefit and share and expand and that is what we ask. Those who are ready are who we want to reach.

Everyone on Earth is at a different level of understanding of the concept of the future of Earth, of their own spirit; all can be given the opportunity to see and hear, but not all will be ready.

The messages are authentic and come from a special source of pure white light energy and needs to touch those who are ready. Messages are given in many ways – simplicity being important in presentation.

Present as given! All need to be given the opportunity

and we want all to be given the opportunity and then the choice is theirs to investigate further or ignore. It is a choice – so spread the information widely.

The Circle of The Light

During meditation, Kay asked "What are we intended to tell people about the existence and purpose of The Circle of The Light, and is it for all to know?" This was the answering message.

Energy from The Circle of The Light of The Love Energy – remember it's the purest energy of all.

We want our message to be passed on. It is how you will all reach for your heavenly stars. It is how the awakening of the collective consciousness will happen. Pass on information to raise vibrations and help with the transition already taking place on Earth. It will accelerate and aid this event.

Our love is an almighty power and this is the sort of power that needs to be experienced and activated in all transactions on Earth. Power is power of the Light. It is almighty as we have said, but it is gentle, understanding, kind. It is nurturing Love Energy. It needs to embrace all actions, calming all souls.

Being awakened to the Light allows our energy to light every prism of the being and the Earth.

It is important to pass on. We're giving information in stages, little by little. All will be shared. Timing is Divine.

Messages of love and guidance

As mentioned in the introduction, these messages are presented in the order received and have been written down as they were given.

Discovery

Take the steps and you will find what you are looking for.

Search far. It is all before you.

Start the journey.

The joy of giving

Giving is not in a monetary sense. Giving is of yourself – sharing what you have, what you are made of with those around you.

Little things are so important. It's the smile, it's the helping hand, it's the kind word, it's the giving of yourself. This is what you need to do.

In doing this, you Light the world. You can feel the kindness that comes from this 'giving' energy. Please give – give those little things. It is then of yourself.

With this you will expand, and in expanding you help the world – not just the one you are giving to. You expand and spread the joy of giving.

Feel the joy – experience it deep within – because it will then be of yourself.

Love energy

The world is going through a great time of change and needs to know about Love Energy. Love Energy needs to be passed on, but before you can pass it on it needs to be understood and recognised.

Every person carries this energy, but not everyone is awakened to it. This energy is of your very essence, it is central to all that you are.

Awaken the soul's craving – be love by being from the heart. Every action, every word, every thought needs to be expressed in love.

Love is never given as a reward. Love is. Love is, it has no boundaries, it has no conditions.

The Light is love. Live your lives from the heart, then your love will be expressed. Be a disciple of the Light; show this Love Energy by living from the heart. Open your hearts to the Light, then the Love Energy is awakened.

The Light

Light is all that is needed. Realise that the Light is within and without you, so love yourself and love all that is about you. Feel the harmony – it radiates from the Light.

The Light is peace, and the Light gives all that is needed. Reach out for the Light always – embrace the Light and feel the harmony. The soul needs the love, it needs the peace and it needs the harmony that comes from the Light.

Open yourselves to this Light. You are the Light – remember you are always the Light. You are One, you are the Light. Feel the Oneness – be at one with the Light. Unite with the Light!

Nurture the Earth

The Earth needs to be nurtured. It is vital to play your part and stop the deterioration of this planet now.

Every time you do a daily action, like turning on a tap, do it with thought, need, so there is more for others. Everything needs to be shared, there needs to be enough for everyone. Use resources wisely, please do not waste. Play your part in taking responsibility for caring for your world.

In caring for the world and playing your part you can halt the waste and you can harness the flow of the Earth's needs, and restore the abundance that there always was on this beautiful planet.

It is not too late to restore Earth's needs. Please play your part, do not waste - restore the balance.

Christmas

Thank you for asking me to talk to you about Christmas, this time of celebration that you join together and remember the birth of Jesus. This is what needs to be celebrated.

He gave to you the opportunity for expansion of your souls, your spirit, your essence. He asked of you kindness, love; awareness of all that you can be and all that is.

The universe is expansive and this part that you are of is just miniscule, but it is a part of the Whole and you are part of the Whole. This is what you need to realise, because the Whole is expansive, encompassing of all and the Light radiates and shines in all.

Christmas should be a time of remembering what was given for you and for all. It is the purest of times represented by the birth of the new, the baby Jesus.

When you gather with your many friends, your family, remember the giving that happened in the beginning – the giving of life, the beginning of new opportunities. Please honour and value what's been given to you when you celebrate Christmas this year.

I ask you to be giving of yourself. Love yourself, love everyone this Christmas. Expand the spirit, let its true love be given. The true spirit of Christmas. The giving and loving – oh please give, please love.

Expand all the time! Oh please expand, please love, please give of yourself this Christmas. Remember the one who gave to you. Please love the spirit within. Please love the spirit without.

Oh thank you so much for the opportunity to give you this love at Christmas.

Patience

Everything happens as and when it's supposed to. It may not seem like that to you!

There is a purpose for every event – teaches you many things from lessons of learning, understanding, needs of others too, feelings of your own.

Patience is required in many situations and is a necessary learning for further development. Remember to be not only patient with the situation, but also to be patient with yourself.

One cannot expect to learn and be all things to all people, all of the time. You can only give what you can to a situation. You do need to apply patience.

Every situation has a purpose for those involved. The people that it directly relates to have learning. The people who support those people have learning and the people who are closely associated with that whole network also need to allow patience and understanding to flow.

I said to you to remember to be patient with yourself. Do not chastise yourself if you feel you have not allowed the patience required for a situation. Remember to learn from the situation. Patience is not an easy thing because so many things are happening at the same time, around a situation, that need to be dealt with as well.

Just remember to learn from every situation. Give as much as you can – at the time. Be as patient as you can. Consider the person, consider the surroundings, consider yourself. That is all we ask!

Courage

Courage comes in many forms. Some may need to use their courage to leave their house, others to climb a mountain. Respect the courage shown no matter the task, because there is a display of faith to undertake a task that is masked by fear. Doubt in one's self causes the doubt and therefore the fear. Release all fear to the White Light of the Divine – show courage by doing this.

Trust and believe that all things can be overcome when you acknowledge and accept that the loving, powerful God that lives without, also lives within you – then all things are possible.

Physical mountains don't need to be climbed to show courage, but the mountains that you have in your mind need to be released to the White Light to be overcome and this takes faith and courage.

Not all acts of courage show the heroism that one on Earth associates with courage. Remember to always follow the Light – this will help every aspect of your life. Show courage and believe in the God without and the God that dwells within you.

Life is precious

All life is really precious. All life needs nurturing.

Help all you can to give all that is needed to comfort, to nurture, to open the heart to all of the possibilities that are there for the taking.

All life has a purpose. All life needs to be loved.

Engage with as many as you can – so that all know what is central to their being.

Humility

Gifts from God are real treasures when accepted with humility. The treasure is for sharing – not for boasting about. It's for sharing and helping to spread the Light.

Use the gifts given to you wisely.

Collective consciousness

Take time to feel the energy that connects all life on Earth and beyond. The energy is pure and quiet – it is of God. Quiet contemplation time allows for this connection to the energy field of pure love, it is so fulfilling for the spirit, soul, essence of the being.

Walk and talk as one and that is what you will be – one, singular. Remember you are part of the Whole – that is of God – and then you are connected with the collective consciousness.

Being connected within this field of pure love opens up endless possibilities; as the energy allows wisdom, love and joy to be injected into any question posed or any task required.

Present yourself in quietness with authenticity of heart and you will be connected to this greatness. Connect regularly through quiet contemplation and with genuine intention and feel the power of pure love help every aspect of your life.

Ask

Heaven helps those that ask. We always are there when you ask. Live every day knowing we are with you when you ask.

Acceptance

Acceptance of the soul is necessary, as this is what you are – perfect and whole, strong, gentle and true to your creator and blueprint. Acceptance brings peace to the soul – needs no forgiveness to be given to the self because that is who you are.

Acceptance and belief in the central-most part of you brings all the harmony that you need. This harmony will allow you to flourish. Self acceptance is so very important to your journey and the progress of your journey on Earth.

This acceptance will make everything so much easier. Heaven is there with all the help that is needed. Trust in your innermost self. Accept yourself for who you are – a wonderful being in Christ.

Compassion

Be in empathy with any presented situation, as this will open up the compassion within that is required to handle any situation. Accessing and engaging a compassionate heart will bring comfort and understanding to the situation so it is dealt with love.

Love is the most important of all the human emotions. Secure love in your beingness and you will not only show and reflect this, but you will firmly plant this energy on Earth.

This energy of love is needed on Earth to make the change in the vibration to lift it and take it on its next progression – without love, it will eventuate not.

Every situation that presents itself needs to be seen through clear eyes that are filled with understanding, acceptance, compassion and love for all. Love is the key to the future of Earth.

Seek within

Events of significance are passed on and form the history of learning and evaluation for those who follow.

Those who seek the truth will find the answer within themselves and that reference material they access in search of the answers will be but a steering star to their inner wisdom.

The God Force is within as well as without – all around, fully encompassing. Recognise, accept and feel the God Force within and you will be at one with everything and energy of the purest kind will emanate from you.

Love yourself as you are; accept all others as they are, for they too are carriers of the God Force. When all accept and acknowledge the God Force – all will be united by love. The power of love will reign and all will be well on Earth.

Prudence

Wise people will exercise prudence in all their dealings in life. A hard thing to do – but very necessary in order to be assured.

When working with spirit, exercise caution when speaking with others. Ensure that they are like minded and ready to grow. Without the readiness, words of wisdom and knowledge will fall on deaf ears and cause concern to the giver – the bearer of the wisdom.

Wisdom is required on Earth at this time and those 'called' need to be aware of the need to not only deliver much needed messages, but to be cautious in their dealings with themselves and those they come in contact with.

It is not an easy path, but it's one that we ask to ensure that Earth meets its requirements to raise energy of love.

Growth of the spirit

It is generally understood that earthly experiences aid the growth of the spirit. Live and experience widely your life opportunities, allowing the growth that will come from each experience.

Child experiences form many opinions, fears – that are carried through to later life, often harming the spirit. Experiences of the child need to be taken in context. Children are vulnerable and some take advantage, and these experiences are carried on in that life. It is so important that these experiences, that have harmed the spirit, are healed.

Healing the spirit means that the human needs to let go of these memories. Trauma at a young age is detrimental to future growth – needs to be released.

Many avenues are available to help – not always known – so many suffer far too long. Spirit, soul, essence healing is vital.

Your heavenly family

Every person living on Earth is born into a family.
Collectively all have a part to play. Individually a part to
play – although when of age and therefore can fend for
oneself – should never think on your own as there is a
collective consciousness – another family – you are
part of a heavenly family.

Make a conscious decision to link to your heavenly
family. Then work together – that is how everything is
achieved.

The collective consciousness – it is when you remember
to be part of the Whole. You have a family and it is not
just here on Earth. It is all around you, it is within you.

When all allow their feelings to be from their highest self
and therefore be from their essence, they will ignite and
unite with the higher consciousness. The more people
who know that their being is more than flesh and bone,
the more people that awaken their spirit, soul, essence,
the more who can connect into the greater
consciousness, then more Light can be radiated from the
heavens to the Earth.

Illumination is what is needed and this comes from the
energy of The Circle of The Light.

Celebrate

Make every day a celebration of your life. Give thanks for your experiences – for through the experiences you will learn to appreciate your connectedness to All That There Is.

There is much need to feel part of all of creation by the spirit within. Awaken each day to really see the greatness you are part of. Embrace it, appreciate it and celebrate it with all your heart.

Give thanks for who you are, love yourself – know your purpose unfolds daily with all the support that you need. Merge with the greatness and celebrate your connectedness.

Universal energy

Draw on the Universal Energy – the source of All. Call on this cosmic power to help.

Forgiveness

The Light within shines brightest when all is in harmony:
body, mind, spirit. Ensure all ingredients for harmony by
allowing forgiveness from the heart.

For all people and situations that interact with your
beingness – forgiveness from the heart, no matter the
cause, brings the deepest sense of wellbeing to the
Light within.

Harbour no ill feelings, resentments, hatred – as this will
stunt the spirit's progress and negate the Light.

Open your heart and allow forgiveness. Progress the
spirit through forgiveness. Bring all of the beingness in
harmony through forgiveness.

Spread love

We ask for messages of love to be spread far and wide. 'Love' being the key to future progress.

Harmony comes from love. Peace comes from love. Love is the lesson to be learnt on Earth.

A genuine emotion is all that is required – must be genuine – must be from the heart. Love is central in All That There Is.

Help us to spread the need for love on Earth now. Love is central to Earth's progression.

Please spread love, genuine love.

Our purpose

Life on Earth is about realising what you are all about. Not only the fleshy body that you see, but you are much more.

Awakening to this knowledge – important for the connection of the humanness with the spirit. The understanding, the importance, of the spirit within – allowing the spirit within to play its part through the heart of the human.

All actions, thoughts and deeds from the human when given through the heart will accomplish what is asked. All connections are needed for the growth; the understanding of the human's journey – the journey to the Light.

The human is not asked to not live its human life. It is asked to realise, on its way to the Light, that it is part of the Light. This acceptance and understanding will enable the journey to be more fruitful.

Explore all that there is in your journey – the laughter, the fun, the disappointments, the successes – know these come as a way of learning about yourself. Learning about yourself and who you really are and what you are part of is what the earthly journey is all about.

Love of the Light is with you all. Always with you! Always waiting to be illuminated more! Nurture your very essence, your spirit, your soul, living your life from the heart and the human experience will be served. Honour yourselves, respect and love yourselves.

Justice

Justice will come from displaying and living from the heart.

Nourish the spirit

Seek with sincerity to nourish the spirit within. The spirit, soul, essence needs unconditional love which will allow the heart to give and receive love.

Being a transmitter and a receptor is the way forward. Balance will prevail when the energy of love is exchanged in all transactions.

Unconditional love is an acceptance of who and what you are inside and outside. Be all that you are – be the human being that you are. Use all your senses to bring joy, happiness, fun and laughter to your existence.

Show your character/personality; be strong; be understanding; be compassionate; speak honest words; be accepting and you will be loving, coming from the heart. A heart that is open through the experiences that nourish it.

Trust the spirit within

When the human heart is at one with itself, the spirit within will be filled with joyous rapture. This will ignite and the spirit will expand connecting with the spirit without, providing much illumination for the human's journey.

Learning to trust the spirit within – then comes with connection to All That There Is – the true pure energy of life.

Human emotions

It is important for the happiness of the soul to experience human emotions, allowing growth from every experience.

Negativity needs to be released for true growth. Fulfilment comes from a happy heart. The soul will be nourished and shine and oneness will come and love will penetrate and emanate all.

Healing

The Light streams in from a wide open door. The flow of the Light is constant and strong and powerful in every way. This Light touches all and when in contact from the Source, all will be so well. 'Well' in all context, not just physically well but well – whole.

The Light shines through healers and will be passed on through the healing touch. Healers at this time on Earth are so important in moving forward – Earth moving forward. Opportunities present themselves. Healing needs to be given.

Many forms of healing are opening up to many on Earth. All need to be accepted, as different beings will be drawn to different things. Important to acknowledge – all healing comes from the Source. So no matter what healing is given, what is selected by the human being – the Source will be the healer.

Moving away from structured ideas on healing methods helps many who can't be helped by conventional methods – remembering that the soul, the spirit, the essence is what needs healing. Awakening the human being, to the concept that healing needs to take place – of the spirit, soul and essence – is what we ask you to do.

Nurturing the soul, spirit and essence allows the growth – allows the Light, the source of All to be alive, bright and active in the human being.

Love energy channellers

Channellers of Love Energy are being activated and being guided to take up their task on Earth. The time is aligned now to the source energy so the spreading of this energy through various healing and teaching practices can now prevail more easily.

All those carrying this encoded energy are venturing upon the task they agreed to many lifetimes ago, and have returned to Earth to ensure the anchoring and expansion of the Love Energy that was seeded in the time of Christ on Earth.

All channellers are being asked to keep communicating with the spirit within and the spirit without and to be open to what is being asked of them. It is time to trust in inner knowingness, bringing the spirit without and the spirit within together in oneness to ensure achievement of task.

Many are awakening to their need to find another way to fill their half full cup – the realisation that there is more to their humaness that needs nurturing and developing. They are seeking the Love Energy Channellers – be ready to help.

Help those that seek

Congratulate all that come in search of themselves. Many will not know what they are really searching for, just that there must be more.

Nurture their inquiringness. Respect the fragile threshold they stand on. Pass on the entrusted pure energy of love through healing and be open to sharing your story. Pass on messages of ours relative to the searcher to give hope and guidance. Encourage all that come to be aware of the part they can play in progressing Earth's transition.

Support for channellers

Much is evolving – many awakening to their true potential – taking the steps that will enhance the magnitude of the energy required for transition.

Much work needs to be done before this event. This is the preparation stage. Guides and helpers are working tirelessly with their channels ensuring good connections, and knowledge is available for those who seek help from the channellers.

This experience is very new to many of the channellers and they need all the guidance they can receive at this time. They need to be willing to be open to receive, allowing the energy and wisdom to flow through easily.

Be in the now

This time is like no other time. It is important to leave the past behind. Earth's continuance is reliant on the current situation.

The role you play of bringing the Love Energy through needs your focus in the now. Your awareness of your inner Light will shine even brighter when you're in the now. Creation's plan being played out on the Earth plane needs all channels to focus on the now. This time when you focus on the now – you will be at peace, at one, with all that you are.

Being in that focus will allow the Love Energy to flow from one to the other, to the next. Being in tune with who you are, knowing all there is to know about you will bring about the greatest change on Earth for all creation.

Ask for love

There is so much love waiting to be given to the Earth at this time.

We need the Earth. We need the people on the Earth to ask for this love to be released – to be given. We see the need. We give when we are asked.

Please ask. We wait to share the love.

Make a difference

Accept that all things come from the Source. Realise you have God-given gifts to use to make a different world. A world where acceptance, understanding, love and peace reigns. This is the energy that will raise Earth to a higher level.

This will only happen if all make a conscious decision to act from the heart level – pouring forth their love energy.

Acknowledge your helpers

Greet on waking and thank before sleeping your 'Spirit Helpers of the Light'. Dwell with them in love and with trust, accepting their guidance to reach fullness of potential.

Create quiet times in your life to hear their call. A mind that is still will be in harmony and will be ready to receive the call.

Be willing to be in the service of the Light.

Enjoy the beauty of creation

Welcome the energy of the elements each day.

Receive refreshment from the cleansing rain and strength from the force of the wind. Let the sun energise and warm you, and let a blanketing of snow provide fun for the child within.

There is beauty and wonderment in all of creation, absorb it and reflect it.

Spiritual growth

Each day the human being enters is an opportunity to explore and discover potentialities:

• Growth for the physical being by participating fully in the human existence.

• Discovery of the spirit within and the ability to connect with the Source of All.

Deal with all physical needs honestly, being true to yourself and those you are responsible to and for. Transact your dealings from the heart to ensure that honesty and sincerity always prevail.

To enable the spirit within to be discovered, nourished and allow expansion, the human being needs to make a conscious decision to explore the inner 'self' – spirituality.

The individual's spiritual journey upon the Earth plane will take different forms, which is to be expected, as all are different! All earnest exploration along the way will be beneficial, nourishing the spirit within, allowing growth little by little as each discovery is acknowledged and awakens the spirit and is accepted by the mind.

Start the journey or continue your journey, as eventually those who truly seek will unite with the spirit without, the Source of All; finding unity, the great Oneness.

Healing Earth

Constant attention is being given to healing channels on Earth at this time. They are so needed to allow the new energy of love to penetrate all those that seek help and their way on their path. The more who receive and are opened, the easier our job will be and the sooner the Earth plane will be healed.

It is not just the people on the Earth that need healing, Earth is crying out for healing at this time. The people on the Earth are responsible for some of the affects on the Earth, but through their knowingness of love they can project themselves as a healing force upon the Earth.

Encourage those who already acknowledge our presence to spread this energy to awaken those around them, because that's how it will spread. It is like the ripple on the water. In the centre it starts, and it moves out and touches the next and the next until the entire pond is full of ripples. This is what we would like to see happen with the energy of love on Earth.

From the heart

If you work from the heart, so many achievements will be made by every individual and that growth of the individual will be shown – it will be displayed – and the example will be before your friends and colleagues and all of your society and this great energy will spread.

Place each day in the hands of your God – the greatness without – that you are a part of and walk your true path with the guidance that is at your side.

Believe in yourself – you will then know who you are.

Love is needed

Love is needed on Earth more than it ever was. It needs to be shown. I've asked you before to show love in your thoughts, actions and deeds. Please continue to do this. Keep trying. Not always the easiest to do, but does so help the Earth in it's time of transition. Love Energy needs to flow. It needs to be the focus of your lives.

Know the value of love

Messages have been extended to you asking for actions to come from the heart. Perhaps we need to clarify this to make it even easier to be understood.

Value love. Give it the highest value, like you value money. Love has the higher value. Actions in the name of love hold all the components because it will allow compassion, understanding, harmony, kindness, the caring – these are the things that hold true value. A bank balance won't do it. The heart holds the power and will supply all that is needed.

We hope this is clear because very important to change the value understanding. We have told you that all life is precious; we have asked you to live from the heart.

We hope that this message clarifies the importance that humankind should place on love.

A message of hope

With the help of all spiritually minded people – and that is everyone – help to raise love's energy on Earth. This is not the first time that this message is being given.

It is so important to express yourselves from the heart. Love is all that is needed to improve the quality of life. Seeing from the heart will always give the right answer.

Please engage in spreading love. Make it your mission! Without love, Earth will cry.

Accept each other

Allow your spiritual development to unfold through all your experiences. When you admire or wonder at the landscape of the world you live in – you are seeing God at work. There is no judgement on your part – just acceptance of what there is – the beauty, the power, the serenity, the strength, the warmth and much, much more.

When you accept that everyone you come in contact with is of God you will accept their differences, see their inner beauty, and see God at work. This is proving for many to be one of the most difficult of tasks.

We ask you to please remember that all on Earth have the God Force energy pulsating through them, and that incarnates want to fulfil their journey.

Each journey although different, needs to be expressed in love and with love and through this practise you will find the ability to accept each other.

Play your part

Much is happening and will continue. It is all to do with the Earth's vibration. It needs help. Earth needs assistance from every member of the human race.

Please play your part – lift the vibrations by doing everything from the heart. The heart and love are the key to the changes that need to be made.

Our message seems desperate because we see so many sad events on Earth and it only needs the love, the action of love, to change the balance.

Help us change the balance. Negativity needs to be released and positivity reign in every being. Let the soul show forth.

About the authors

Kay Meade is a trance medium who has been channelling messages from the 'Circle of The Light of The Love Energy', a group of spiritual beings, since mid 2009.

Kay and husband Peter Ashley practice and teach Reiki in New Zealand.

For further information about the authors, their books and meditation CDs, and the latest messages from The Circle of The Light of The Love Energy go to www.earthmessagepress.com.

The authors welcome any feedback or questions related to this book at www.earthmessagepress.com/contact-us.

Books by the authors include.
Love is the Key
Poems for You

You have everything that you need

It is so important for me to impart to you that you are a being filled with the God Force.

You are attached to All That There Is and you are full of love. You have everything you need. You are not asked to do anything that you cannot achieve. All that is necessary is to draw on the inner self, the God Force within.

Allow the spirit, soul, essence of the self to show forth and love will be with you. You can achieve all that you need to do. Come from within and connect with without.

Abundance

Within each human being upon Earth, abundance dwells. It is in the form of love. Love abides with you. It is God given. It is the inner spirit, soul, essence – is connected to the spirit without and provides all that is needed.

Abundance is with you all. It will be realised when the spirit within is nurtured and through the searching that you are doing now, you are nurturing the spirit. So abundance will flourish for you in every possible way.

Continue with your search; with the nourishment of the soul and you will know who you are and the rewards, by way of your God-given gifts being realised, will be before you.

Mother's love

Mothers give their children love and they nurture them until they can become themselves.

A mother's love is never seen to be depleted and yet it can be when love is not returned by the child.

Earth is the mother of all humankind and it has been giving of itself over and over again. It is now time for humankind to return the love to Earth – its mother, in order for it to continue.

Take up arms and help the Earth – for you need it. It is time to say thank you and love Earth – your mother.

Blend

Blend; blend the inner life and the outward and come together as one – the spirit unite. The outward daily life has a purpose, as it will reveal the inner spirit.

Love all living things

Every living thing deserves love – needs to be seen with compassionate eyes. Understanding needs will help love spread.

Eyes of compassion often are associated with how animals are seen because of the loyalty that is given unquestionably, and yet is not given to fellow human beings.

See every living thing with the tenderness that you see the delicate, the fragile, the friendly, welcoming, heart-warming animal.

Separate yourself not

Separate yourself not from the spirit – you are one. The power of the spirit is available to you, so work with the spirit to achieve your aims.

Work with your spirit guides

Agreeing to work with your spirit guide or guides is a most valuable 'marriage' that is available for you to enter, at any age, whenever you are ready.

You will know when you are ready, your soul, spirit, essence will hear or sense the need and the call.

Commit to this union with all your love, trust and loyalty and you will be in the service of the Light, a channel of love upon the Earth.

Opportunities will be presented to you that will give much to you as you give to the Light and realise your potential.

Be all that you are

Seek only to be all that you are. Only all that you are –
there is nothing else to be.

Our gift

In this book is our gift to all Earth beings. This will give guidance, allowing all who read this gift such an opportunity of fulfilment. This is the beginning, this is where the expansion begins and then the golden rain will give nourishment and Light.